THE INSPIRATIONAL ALTER-EGO

MOVEMENT

BY

Ebony Mitchell

INSPIRATIONAL ALTER-EGO MOVEMENT

The two images are of the author/the purpose seeker passing the pen to herself symbolizing her alter ego coming together to tell her story and aligning with who she has become now, looking up to God to lead her in writing. They are becoming as one writing this book. Embracing everything about her life. The alter-ego part of her with the hidden face covered by the hat is giving her permission to write their story as she passes the pen back. They are wearing the same clothing to represent them becoming as one, Ebony Teron Alexander-Mitchell.

A LETTER FROM THE EDITOR

Ebony Teron Alexander Mitchell, who knew this small in stature, soft-spoken young woman had a big voice to write such a riveting documentary. The Inspirational Alter-Ego Movement filled with excellent content and passion, pulls the reader inside the story. The author singles out and directs the reader to refocus. The documentary is compelling and captivating; I could hardly wait for the next segment. Ebony hit the nail on its proverbial head putting this documentary together. The book is picturesque and very powerful. Ebony mastered the art of her passion, photography. You need to see for yourself how the skills of photography testimonials leap off the pages. Hands-down, this documentary will appear on the silver screen. You may find yourself in the portraits of passion throughout the documentary. Forget the fact Ebony grew up in a small town, and we know her personally. You will be hard-pressed to find a more detailed and thorough book on the topics in the documentary. Ebony speaks with simple eloquence, making the stories easy to follow; she has a heart for the people. Ebony, I am a person of words; take a bow because you deserve it. Your work is powerful. I enjoyed every word, photograph, and segment.

--Elder Veronica Mayfield

INTRODUCTION

This is a book of Salvation, Healing, and Deliverance through the journey of the Inspirational Alter-Ego Movement. This movement displays through a Visual Testimonial Portrait. The movement captivates the reader as each participant tells their wilderness story and utilizes God's word through scriptures and spiritual songs.

This book is meant to reach all ages: the lost and weary Christians; people who are unsure of their faith, blind and deaf, and multicultural. This book will be used as an encyclopedia to reference a period in life you may be going through. The reader can simply flip through the book, see portraits, hear audio versions, and read their way out of struggles.

All learners, visual, auditory, reading/writing, and kinesthetic, will have access. This book will give people comfort and hope for tomorrow, knowing they are not alone and will overcome every obstacle with God!

ACKNOWLEDGMENTS

Mary, a Jack & Jill mom, asked me to make a slideshow/video with pictures of our year and the children of all the cultural, educational, and social activities, thus capturing the Jack & Jill purpose in our ENC Chapter. I did not realize it then, however, looking back, I enjoyed the creativity of making the video of pictures. I quickly learned the editing program.

Jack & Jill's mothers Tracy and Lisa were so caring during my first miscarriage in Greenville, NC. I am forever grateful to them and for seeing greatness in me.

To all of the JnJ mothers, thank you for showing me what making friends your family really mean, even if you are not blood related.

My husband, Nick, thank you for staying with me through the tough times. Even when you did not understand how to help me, you were there. In addition, I will always love you for that.

My daughters, Lyrik, Destiny Maleah, Emori, and Joy, thank you for teaching me to be your mom. Each of you has such unique gifts. I encourage you to use them all and always seek God for the strategies to implement them. I love you with my whole heart.

Dad, thank you for giving your wisdom, and I really was listening. I love you!

Mommy, thank you for your style and class, and most importantly, for helping me to understand spiritual gifts. You taught me to stand up for myself and not to take anyone's mess.

IAE team, thank you for helping me bring this vision to life. I could not have succeeded without any of you. My husband, Nick, and Illustrator Michelle "Mickey" Alexander, Mua Teresa Faulk, Tika Griffin, and all the overcomers, who so willingly told their stories in this book.

I thank you, God, my creator, the one who knew me and did not give up on me. I am eternally grateful to who so graciously allowed me to see a glimpse of the life He has for me. I will forever live a life of gratitude and give YOU the honor and the glory YOU so deserve!

TABLE OF CONTENTS

[CHAPTER 1]—THE PURPOSE SEEKER

DELIVERANCE

This book highlights the details of my personal life journey and how I became the person, I am today. This story depicts others' lives whose testimonies catapult them and me into triumph and victory. The phrases "It takes a village, and no man is an island" are deeply rooted in black culture. History tagged us quoting the ever-popular phrase "We are our brother's keeper!" It is incredible how God aligned the lives of everyone in this book to tell the story of HIS love. Each from different backgrounds, exemplifying strength through pain, perseverance, friendship, and most of all, through faith. The common factor we all realized is there is purpose in our pain. Hence the name…The Purpose Seeker.

I graduated from high school with the optimism to become a Pediatric Doctor. I was determined not to let anything stop me. Just call me focused! I could make the right choices every time; little did I know God had another plan. Therefore, I went off to college, graduated with a B.S. in Biology, a Minor in Chemistry, and went off to Chiropractic school.

My idea of a career changed from a Pediatric Doctor to a Physical Therapist, then finally to a Chiropractor. I fell in love with the human anatomy and looked forward to my practice one day. Again, little did I know another child was in the plan. Feeling overwhelmed and alone, I decided to withdraw from Doctorate school to care for my two children. I started purpose seeking, re-evaluated my choices thus far, and began brainstorming ways to get back on track with my plan.

I grew up with two great parents in a loving and godly home. Therefore, I knew I had to start making choices that would brighten my future and everyone who depended on me. I married my college sweetheart and soulmate, which I learned later, God ordained us together. We had three beautiful daughters at the time, and our unforeseen blessing was to come. I will speak on that blessing later in my story. This part of my life consisted of working and providing for my family. However, I always knew God purposed more for me than this. When you are unfulfilled, nothing will validate the hunger in your spirit and soul.

I spent day after day frustrated. When could I go back to fulfilling my dreams while waiting for my husband to finish school and find his dream career? Finally, after a few years of the same routine, my husband received a job that required us to relocate to another state, Greenville, N.C. We were both excited and nervous at the same time. Overjoyed, my husband knew that he could give our family more, and we would have a new start with his job. However, the excitement soon faded. We started to have challenges in our marriage, not realizing what we faced. [*God will show you who you are as you seek HIS will for your life*].

The life we faced left only one option, God. I became completely broken. My husband and I struggled with past hurts, forgiveness, losing a job, and to add insult to injury, dealing with the first of my two miscarriages. I had a feeling of abandonment. For a while, my three girls and I attended church alone.

Standing at the altar seeking guidance and wondering where to go from here. Hurt and confused, praying for strength. The scripture says *prayers of the righteous avails much*. I needed someone to pray for me through this trial. God validated HIS love for me as the church's prayer warriors took my three girls and me before the Lord.

I did not understand. I asked God, "What am I not getting; what is it I am not understanding? I am going to church, and I pray daily. I try to be the best mom and wife. But, God, please tell me, what am I missing?" I was not fulfilling my purpose, and it tore me apart! My family and friends thought I was living the so-called good life of a stay-at-home mom. To them, it appeared as if I had it all together; however, deep inside was a pale, lost person, mentally confused. I was not eating. I had suicidal thoughts and even an attempt. I remember once running a whole tub of bathwater, I wanted to go under, but my husband came in just in time. Looking back, I never wanted to leave this physical earth; I only wanted someone to see me! Suicidal tendencies were my cries for help. Finally, God cleansed and healed my husband and me, so we could fulfill HIS purpose and plans for our lives. Today, I advocate for Suicide Awareness and participate in a yearly walk with my family.

[**Post-partum depression (PPD), also called post-natal depression, is a mood disorder associated with childbirth, affecting both sexes. Symptoms may include extreme sadness, low energy, anxiety, crying episodes, irritability, and changes in sleeping or eating patterns**].

Undiagnosed and unknowingly, I suffered through these emotions for several years after my childbirths.

I often wondered why no one saw me. Of course, I would be there for family and friends, but I could not talk about my insecurities with anyone. In a crowd of people and not one person realized my emptiness. Behind the façade of a smiling face, I just wanted to be honest. I wanted to take off the mask, come naked and unashamed, not literally, to tell anybody who would listen about my troubles. I knew God would listen to me because I grew up in church. Therefore, I carried the loneliness I felt inside to the only go-to place I knew, the church. I kneeled before God, praying and believing that HE would make things better…and HE did.

I began to meet pillars of the community, women, doctors, lawyers, and educators, much like the careers I had in mind. Moreover, I met their families and built new relationships. Finally, however, I knew God's voice from the yearning I felt in my heart; it was time to move back home to Lancaster, S.C. Therefore, four years passed, and we did just that, packed our belongings, my husband quit his job, and we moved home.

[When two of you get together on anything at all on earth and make a prayer of it. My father in heaven goes into action. And when two or three of you are together because

of me, you can be sure that I'll be there. Matthew 18:19-20 MSG]

We did not know where our next meal would come from, but we trusted God. We had a rental property, and we lived around family. Jobless for six months, we did not go hungry, neither did we lack in any area of our lives. When we dropped our plans for God's plans, we realized that HE would indeed care for us. My favorite cripture: **[But they that wait upon the Lord shall renew their strength; they shall mount up with wings as eagles. They shall run, and not be weary, and they shall walk, and not faint. Isaiah 40:31 KJV]** this scripture described the moment in my life.

SELF-MOTIVATION

I had to self-motivate. Time for me to start a new journey. A new way of thinking, a new way of being, no more crying, no more anger, no more catering to my feelings. It is a new day! If you have to cry sometime, then cry! Just keep it moving, wipe your tears, and do not quit. After all, you are a Kings' Kid!

I had to relearn my identity. My first name, **Ebony**, means firm African root that is royalty. A girl's name of English origin means intensely black wood. African American parents because of its connotations of blackness and beauty favored the name. Trending down since the 80's, according to Wikipedia. My middle name **Teron** means you develop high spirituality, as you have God's protection. You are sensitive, affectionate, imaginative, and cooperative, spiritually aware, and prone to self-sacrifice. You can keep secrets, a good diplomat, and may have healing and psychic powers. You have an eventful and exciting life. Teron also means versatility and the ability to comprehend. The desire to lead, inspire and control others' affairs. Teron suggests giving, courage, being bold, and being action oriented. Someone energetic, strong-willed, and wants to make a difference in the world. This attitude often attracts you to cultural interests, politics, social issues, and cultivating your creative talents (Wikipedia).

From the womb, God established greatness inside; I just had to tap into it. As a result, God renewed my strength. My spiritual eyes and ears were more in tune than ever. Daily I heard God clearly either through song or divine intervention. God instructed my husband and me to leave my home church, a difficult decision for us, but we are following God's path now. He led us to serve at Faith, Hope, and Victory Church, another local ministry in the area. Here, our spiritual gifts grew, as well as my husband accepting the call to preach the gospel. I sang in the choir and God opened the door for me to do what I love, photography. Who knew there would be a place in the church to utilize my passion? I certainly did not. My photography gift fell in place like a piece of a puzzle.

How did my parents know I would excel in this profession? I liked taking pictures, not really looking for it to be a career; however, God knew. **[I know the plans I have for you, says the Lord. Jeremiah 29:11 NLT]** A hint to parents…always consult the Lord about your children. He already has a master plan for them.

I remember the first Polaroid camera my parents bought me.

The kind where the pictures would slide out as soon as you take them. I took boxes of photos with that camera. Although it seems like a lifetime ago, that camera is ancient, unlike today's digital cameras. Nevertheless, it is one of my prized possessions, and I still have it today. That ole Polaroid camera is symbolic. A constant reminder to consult God for His plans for our life before we make our own; accepting what God says about our life makes things much more manageable. Lesson learned! I believe we know early on what our gifts and purpose are; however, we allow circumstances, and the opinion of others influence our paths. So, hold on to your childhood ambitions and dreams; therein lies the keys to your future when you become an adult.

My childhood passion for photography began to manifest. People in the church started asking my husband and me to take pictures of their special events. Therefore, we named them *"Amillion and One Blessings."* Finally, we decided to make it official. In 2014, my husband and I established the photography and video imaging business known as *Amillion & 1 Photography & Video Imaging*. God turned my passion into a business! I settled into my role as The Boss and an entrepreneur, something I always wanted. I continued my daily prayer time with the Lord as I usually did.

FULFILLED PURPOSE

Living within my purpose caused me to seek the face of God for instruction. However, first I needed to know how God planned to use me in this business.

One sunny fall day, I was riding along, looking at the change of season's scenery. Then, I crossed under the bridge on Old Kershaw Camden 521 highway. I heard God speak plainly to me, "Ebony, you are stronger now, and I want you to do a portrait of your testimony. And I want you to call it The Inspirational Alter-Ego Movement." WOW! I should have stopped and pulled my car over when God gave me the vision, instead, I kept driving in amazement! God spoke explicitly and in detail about how the vision would look. God knows the gifts and talents He placed in us; I am a visual learner, and what He instructed was perfect for me. Well, I could not do the portrait of myself, but my husband, who believed in the vision, was right there; he supported me every step of the way. The idea God gave me required putting a team of mentors together. People who are knowledgeable in the areas I lacked. I am forever grateful to the

17

men and women God used to bring this vision to fruition. Photography and video imaging have many aspects; therefore, the business continues to grow. Salvation, healing, and deliverance, the movement's primary focus, remain the central theme in all the photoshoots.

God tremendously graced my life. With HIS goodness and the testimonies of others, I am an overcomer.

[The Inspirational Alter-Ego Portrait – Me, who you see on the outside versus the inner me, who the world does not see, that I deal with daily. The inspirational portrait depicts life as an overcomer by staying connected to the source, God].

IAE MOVEMENT LEVERAGE PROGRAM

I leverage the program to achieve my career aspirations, having peace of mind, the freedom of creativity, and the joy of growing and learning. Leveraging allows me to live in my purpose and inspire others to do the same. I will accomplish this by:

- Hosting workshops
- Teaching money management, how to start and maintain a successful business, and
- Learn the art of photography
- Making lives better one photoshoot at a time.

Isaiah 40:31

But they that wait upon
the Lord shall renew their strength:
they shall mount up with wings as eagles:
they shall run, and not be weary; and
they shall walk, and not faint.

THE PURPOSE SEEKER IAE PORTRAIT

The first image – I was broken. Sitting on the floor, head down, pale skin, and sad heart.

Words describing how I felt inside. I envisioned holding onto a rope symbolizing my prayers to God.

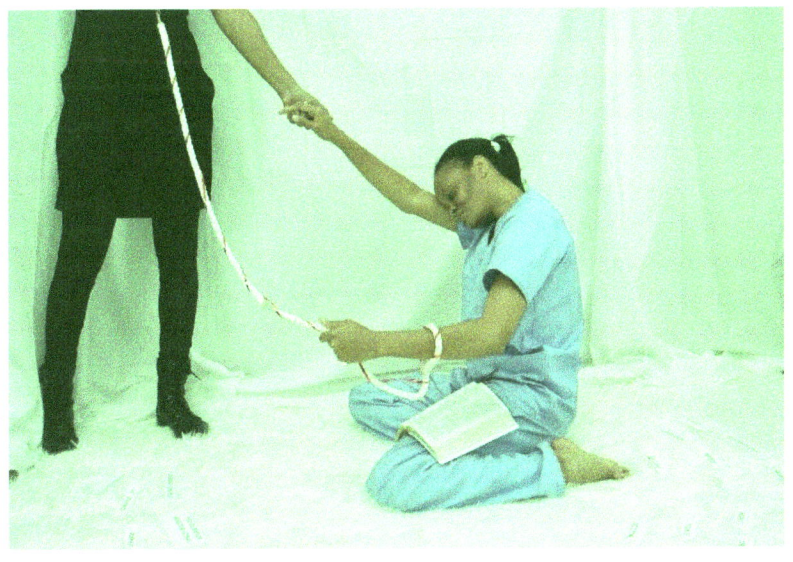

The second image – A strong and powerful woman, full of energy, flare, and style looking up to God. Holding the first image hand, expressing with God, we will rise again, together. The wings on her back symbolize her character of strength, like an eagle. The rope represents a connection to God, who was always present in her life. The storms of life interfered with her hearing God clearly, although she knew HE was there, somewhere. My breakthrough songs were "Fill me up again and

Better Days." I needed God's knowledge and HIS ways of handling world issues.

The process of the shoot brought a sense of peace, freedom, joy, and strength. Knowing that I was living in my purpose and inspiring others to do the same. Before the final stage of my breakthrough, I inflicted pain on myself mentally. I discovered pain is simply weakness trying to exit the body. It could not exist with the strengths God already placed inside; it had to go! Realizing it was not about me; it was bigger than I was.

Jesus came into this world to demonstrate how we can live a sinless life. However, when they crucified HIM, it reminded us of the struggles in life we also have to endure. HE did not leave us empty-handed with no way to win. HE left us a book of testimonies, the Bible, which is our manual for life. As this movement continues, our stories are not only about us; they are inspirations to help others along the way.

THE DREAMER

Produce what is honest to you. God made me in HIS image. Stop worrying about the world's perception of you and focus on what God says. Be mindful of the energy around you; reach your goals and be authentically you! Foster the life given to your children at birth. God's desires for you are wealth, health, faith, and a sound mind. It will lead you to the place where you can hear HIM again.

SALVATION

[Romans 10:9,KJV; that if thou shalt confess with thy mouth the Lord Jesus, and shalt believe in thine heart that God hath raised him from the dead, thou shalt be saved. For with the heart man believeth unto righteousness; and with the mouth confession is made unto salvation.]

I experienced my first and actual encounter with the Holy Spirit singing on Genesis Mass Choir. We traveled on a tour bus to places that included Washington D.C. and various cities around the country. During one of our concerts, the choir sang, "No greater love," led by a beautiful mother in the choir. I remember feeling the Holy Spirit as she sang.

The choir was singing in the seats behind the pulpit, where the congregation had a great view of everyone. The mother sang out of her soul! I started crying, not tears of sadness, but of joy. I finally knew God intimately, and I was singing for HIM. Singing gives me pleasure. I accepted Christ as a teenager. The evening God saved me; we were at a church in downtown Lancaster, S.C. They provided an altar call to everyone desiring salvation. Several people walked to the altar before me, and I went last. The minister laid hands on everyone's head, and most were falling backward on the floor. When it came my time, the minister laid his hands on my head and prayed. After he finished, I thought I was supposed to fall backward on the floor like everyone else. I was very tickled and laughed aloud. I laid there and felt nothing but peace, knowing God saved me.

I was not crying like everyone else. I opened one eye while I lay there on the burgundy-reddish carpet to see what was happening. Someone in the congregation saw me and started to grin. I wondered what to do now; I felt silly laying there, but I knew deep down I was saved. Therefore, I slowly stood up and walked back to my seat. Now that I am maturing in the faith, I realize nothing is wrong with my worship of God. Everyone is different, and that is totally ok. God knows our hearts. Humble yourself and come to HIM just the way you are HE already loves you!

IAE INSPIRATIONS/LIFE LESSONS

Stories that helped the photographer

- Be happy; it aids your healing. If you believe in deliverance, you can overcome anything, even barrenness.
- The My Joy poem. Watching this little girl grow and inspire me is a blessing. I needed her. She is full of joy. She is smiling from the moment she wakes up in the morning until going to bed at night. (Late at night). One day we decided to go hiking up Crowder's Mountain. Joy is probably three years old at the time. The family, trying to make it to the top of the mountain, was all tired. However, Joy kept saying, Mommy, we got this; let's keep going." I kept trying to pick Joy up and carry her because I knew her little legs were tired. "No, mommy, I want to walk," she said adamantly. Surprisingly, she walked the entire three hours until we reached the top of the mountain.
- Sincerely, Joy is a gift to me. She reminds me daily life is a blessing and a joy to live, so enjoy every moment!
- Do not be afraid of the God in you. Read this famous quote by Marianne Williamson "*My deepest fear is not*

that we are inadequate. Our deepest fear is that we are powerful beyond measure."

➢ Manifest, make every vision clear, and every creative idea God gives you. Preparation brings order to bless other people and make them feel good.

➢ Worship God with your life.

➢ Elevate your craft and pave the way. Allow yourself to grow with grace.

The Purpose Seeker's Mom and Dad, Sidney and Etta

➢ Fight for yourself as hard as you fight for others. My dad brought to my attention how I always support everyone, pouring into their dreams and businesses…why are you not pouring into your own?" Wow! I stepped back and pondered what my dad had said. WOW! Dad is right! I looked in my closet and found t-shirts with slogans and the businesses of people in my circle; however, I did not have one of my own.

➤ The source of your limitation is your attachments. Who has connected themselves to you? I prayed and asked God for wisdom, knowledge, and discernment to know the people I should join to partner with in business. I believe it is nice to support others, and we should. However, suppose you are drowning inside and not pouring into your vision. In that case, the potential is there to lose yourself and your purpose. My mommy implied the same thing. One time, she and I were out shopping. I picked up an item I wanted and decided to put it back. "Why did you do that?" my mom said. I told her, "Mom, my family comes first." That really hit me! Self-care is essential. I forgot the benefits and the importance of nurturing.

➤ Sit with God; allow HIM to identify your gifts; and how to use them. Then, HE gives life strategies to whoever asks HIM.

➤ Speak life to yourself; rest often to avoid stress. Journal your emotions, what you are feeling, and seek therapy, or both.

[Interactive questions for the reader to complete after each IAE testimony]

How did the testimony of this overcomer touch your heart, and can you relate?

_____

_____

_____

What was your first impression of the visual IAE portrait? What is it saying to you, and how does it make you feel?

_____

_____

_____

What lesson(s) did you learn?

_____

_____

_____

How can you use this testimony to understand, find your purpose, or continue your walk with Christ?

_____

_____

_____

[CHAPTER 2] — THE BELIEVER

THE PORTRAIT OF THE BELIEVER

[If you can believe all things are possible. Mark 9:23 KJV] we are often told just believe whenever the chips are down. When your back is against the wall, just have faith, they say. Some will question your belief when you feel hopeless. What do you do, left alone with your thoughts, feeling forsaken? In the words of the believer, she said, "Trust God!" This next story is riveting.

As the believer told her story/testimony, immediately a spiritual visualization appeared to me. First, I saw her on the floor surrounded by her emotions fear, infertility, loss, and birth medication. Then staring at the ultrasound photo of her live unborn child. However, later, gazing at the image in disbelief, there is no longer a child in her womb. Even though she is a believer, the feeling of loss and wanting to question God overwhelmed her. The hurt is unbearable. Broken and in despair, how would she go on without her baby. Yet, six weeks or six months, the bond between mother and child develops immediately. You do not quickly shake this kind of loss.

Swiftly, in her second pose, the visualization changed, as you see in the picture. I began to get a visual of a strengthened woman. A beautiful, healthy, pregnant woman consoling the mother who previously suffered the loss of her child. Touching her shoulder and reassuring her, God never leaves us in a valley of despair. In addition, she is not alone. She encouraged her not to give up; there is still a chance in the future of bearing children. The curse of barrenness is not a part of her life. The words of encouragement took effect. So strong with deliverance, the believer begins to encourage herself and stand on the word of God. **["Sing, O barren, thou that didst not bear; break forth into singing, and cry aloud, thou that did**

not travail with child: for more of the children of the desolate than the children of the married wife, saith the Lord." Isaiah 54:1 – 3 KJV]

The believer would sing songs of faith, precisely as the word of God instructed. Restoring her belief in the promises of God. Moreover, the believer confessed astounding statements of faith, like, "My babies are in heaven. I just need to call them down from heaven back to me." WOW! What an inspiration! Talk about crazy faith; this is it. Believing without seeing. Reflecting on the first visual of the ultrasound with the baby, then, without. God gave her renewed hope. **["Now faith is the substance of things hoped for and the evidence of things not seen." Hebrews 11:1 KJV]** the believer's testimony inspired

The Purpose Seeker to believe again. I am not barren, and the few miscarriages did not defeat me. Yes, I am more than a conqueror…I am an overcomer!

"THE BELIEVER"

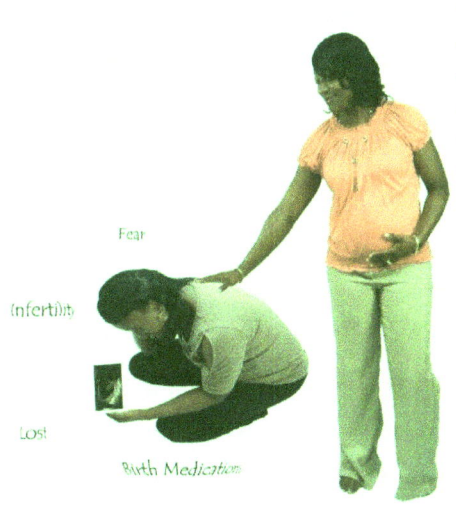

Fear

(Infertil)it

Lost

Birth Medication

[Interactive questions for the reader to complete after each IAE testimony]

How did the testimony of this overcomer touch your heart, and can you relate?

_____

_____

_____

What was your first impression of the visual IAE portrait? What is it saying to you, and how does it make you feel?

_____

_____

_____

What lesson(s) did you learn?

_____

_____

_____

How can you use this testimony to understand, find your purpose, or continue your walk with Christ?

_____

_____

_____

[CHAPTER 3] — MY JOY

This is the new chapter in my story, My Joy. My husband and I overcame barrenness. God blessed us with another daughter who, by the spirit, we named Joy. Thus, Joy Elisabeth Mitchell, we celebrate a great blessing, born, February. 8, 2017. The program from our baby shower celebration had this inscription below

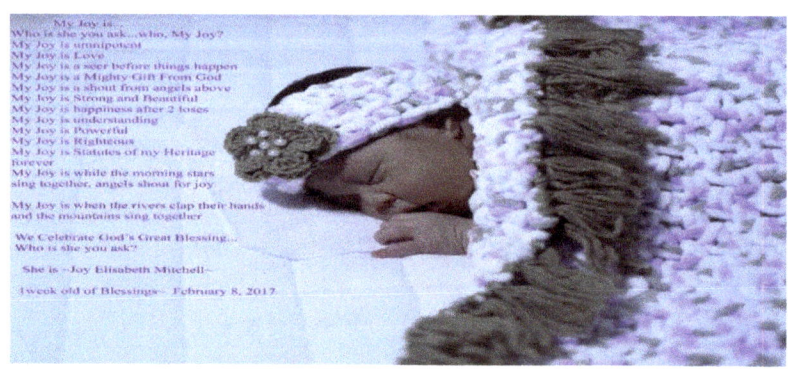

My joy is, who is she, you ask; who is my joy? My joy is characterized as the love we feel from our Omnipotent God; my joy is love; my joy is a seer before things happen; my joy is a mighty gift from God; my joy is a shout from angels above; my joy is strong and beautiful; my joy is happiness after two losses; my joy is understanding; my joy is powerful; my joy is righteous; my joy is statutes of my heritage forever; my joy is while the morning stars sing together and angels shout for joy;

my joy is when rivers clap their hands, and the mountains sing together. Who she is, you ask? She is Joy Elisabeth Mitchell.

What is in a name? She is exactly what her name means. The original spelling, Joi, means a quick, clever mind capable of grasping and assimilating new ideas even in a different spelling. The spelling Joi is a French baby name that means rejoicing. The common spelling Joy means delight and great pleasure, which derives from Middle English and the Old French, Joie.

PRECIOUS JOY

My Joy and I have a routine at bedtime. Every night preparing for bed, she and I would pray the very familiar prayer "Our father who art in heaven…" We all said that prayer with our little ones. My joy would repeat after me all the words in the prayer. One night as we kneeled to pray, My Joy said, "Mommy let me say the prayer tonight." My three-year-old little girl said the most touching and heartfelt prayer; I believe I ever heard. While she prayed, all I could do was look at her in amazement. She said these words:

With gratitude and thankfulness, she says, "Thank you, God, for loving us, thank you, God, for keeping us, and thank you, God, for protecting us. Thank you, God, for keeping us brave; thank you, God, for everything. Thank you, God, for giving us Jesus. Thank you, God, for giving us all your love in Jesus' name. Amen. I genuinely believe God gifted her to me to bring joy back into my heart.

I learned lessons and experienced things I never thought I would have to endure. I know now that you only have to follow Christ and listen to HIM. Ask questions, and HE will lead and guide you daily with the HOLY SPIRIT. God said, "*My yoke is easy, and my burden is light*" *Matthew* **11:30 KJV**. HE will lessen the burdens when we surrender to HIS will for our lives. I hope and pray that I inspired you to continue this journey called life. I pray you will endure with strength and humility and start anew with wings as Eagles!

How did the testimony of this overcomer touch your heart, and can you relate?

_____

_____

_____

What was your first impression of the visual IAE portrait? What is it saying to you, and how does it make you feel?

_____

_____

_____

What lesson(s) did you learn?

_____

_____

_____

How can you use this testimony to understand, find your purpose, or continue your walk with Christ?

_____

_____

_____

[CHAPTER 4] — THE WIFE

THE PERFECT BRIDE OF ARTISTRY

The first encounter with the perfect bride of artistry was one of warmth, caring, loving, positivity, and an inspiring spirit. She tells the story of being a perfectionist, a single mother, and becoming a bride.

Jesus, the only perfectionist, sets the guidelines for our lives. We seek His ways as we strive to be more like Him. We do not have to pretend for God. He meets us right where we are and speak to us on the level of our understanding. In her story, the bride sought Him at a pivotal point in her life. She struggled with her life's dual roles, from being the best mother to transitioning to best wife. Being too independent often got in the way of balancing her roles, and it caused her to struggle. The picture shows the struggle of both positions. Sometimes, the face reveals the pains of our hearts. That is why the ible tells us to look unto God, the Author and Finisher of our faith.

THE WIFE, PERFECT BRIDE OF ARTISTRY

The perfect bride of artistry looks inside the word to find the solace longing in her heart. The Divine intervention and criptures were included in her path to healing and wholeness. The portrait illustrates the various facets of healing, pain, insecurity, guilt, stress, and loneliness. Followed by the queen rising, conqueror, and finally victorious. I noticed she posed artistically, without me coaching her, for each stage of her life with uplifted hands, giving praise and thanks to God.

- The first pose – The strong, perfect, and independent mom. Growing up in a consistent drill sergeant-like environment and organized household, she adopted that behavior and implemented it in her own home.

- The second pose – The beginning of the transition. The dating period of the artistic bride and the soon-to-be husband. Unsure of the longevity of the relationship yet trusting the process to see where it would lead.

- The final pose – The bride. I envisioned the bride thinking…now what? She wants to be a Godly wife but struggles with balancing her dreams with the dreams and lifestyle of her husband.

Throughout the photo shoot, the artistic bride identified areas of her life that needed healing. She had to address her perfectionist spirit. How to organize her creative ideas and how to become the wife God predestined for her. I am amazed that through the camera lens, things you are dealing with can be unveiled. While healing takes place, our spiritual eyes come opened to see things differently and ultimately overcome the issues that held us back far too long.

God is good…do you hear me? I learned two things from the artistic bride story. First, you could have many gifts and talents and not know what to do with them. However, if you seek God, He will help you organize and use your skills and have all your talents working together for the greater good.

We must use all our gifts. Assisting the world helps us fulfill our purpose. Like the bride, God gave her the talent of modeling; however, she could lose it without understanding.

I learned the importance of maintaining your identity as a woman, even in marriage. This is because a woman not only has the responsibilities of a wife; she also must carry out the God-given purposes for her life.

As the rib that holds everything together, marriage and the family, we are equipped and built for it. These tasks appear overwhelming, but honestly, women, we can do it. God prepared us with everything needed to be successful in every area. His guidance helps us overcome every obstacle if only we ask for HIS assistance. From the wife of artistry, I learned to focus on one creative idea at a time. Perfect one thing before you add on something else.

The thing that keeps me grounded is my perspective and mindset to take one day at a time. One day, one task, one creative idea at a time. This way, I remained centered and able to complete that one thing before going to the next and avoiding incompleteness. The beauty of completeness is worth focusing on that one thing. Then, you can fully witness the manifestation of the gifts and talents God gave you.

The wife of artistry had to transition from being an independent single mother and provider for her daughter to a wife depending solely on her husband. I could imagine this being difficult for anyone in her shoes. However, the artistic wife adapted and moved forward; she was already equipped. She just needed to tap into it.

For her, it meant blocking outside influences. Doing so, she started to seek God intently. Finding out from God, what a wife should be, and the more she sought after HIM, He filled her with wisdom. Thus, making her more vital as a wife and a woman. The scriptures that got the artistic wife through the perfectionist phase and the battles with anxiety are Matthew 11: 28 – 30 and Isaiah 41:10. Also seen in the IAE portrait of "The Perfect Bride of Artistry."

Isaiah 41:10 *For the Struggle.*
Matthew 11:28-30 *For the Renewal.*

How did the testimony of this overcomer touch your heart, and can you relate?

_____

_____

_____

What was your first impression of the visual IAE portrait? What is it saying to you, and how does it make you feel?

_____

_____

_____

What lesson(s) did you learn?

_____

_____

_____

How can you use this testimony to understand, find your purpose, or continue your walk with Christ?

_____

_____

_____

[CHAPTER 5]— THE VICTORIOUS SURVIVOR

NO MORE BULLYING

The moment I met him, I felt strength and joy in his spirit. He had a smile and a humble heart that would brighten anyone's day. In his story, he and others were playing at a friend's house around the pool. Another kid came from behind and poured boiling hot water all over his body, causing severe burns. During his photo shoot, I saw the braveness and urgency within him to be a light for his peers. Yet, regardless of what he went through, the determination to advocate for teenagers like himself is admirable.

Of his poses, they exemplify neither weakness nor struggle. He survived a harsh burn attack at the hand of a bully that put him in the hospital. However, my spirit of discernment could not let him pose in the same image of his burns. It would not let me put him back into a state of vulnerability. Instead, I saw a warrior, and a survivor, so I photographed him as such. I envisioned him victorious. The scars were no longer visible, and I visualized him defeating the bully who tried to take away his joy but failed.

- The first pose is of the survivor portraying the bully who victimized him. Laying on the ground holding a pot of hot water and a facial expression of anger.

- In the second pose, I saw him stepping on the bully with one foot and arms folded. Again, displaying strength and muscles as if defeating the enemy, winning a wrestling match, or overcoming his opponent, the devil.

- The victorious survivor mentioned his dad's faith inspired him to fight through his pain. A particular phrase in his story stayed with me. He said, "Be happy. If you are happy, you heal faster." That is precisely what he did while in the hospital, remain happy and receive healing. Throughout his journey, he often sang this with his dad, "God's got a blessing with my name on it." The song encouraged them to both keep going and believe in his healing.

God definitely has a blessing with his name on it, especially in front of his peers and the world. The bible says, *"Your gifts will make room for you and bring you before kings."* The victorious survivor is the strongest, wisest, and bravest teenager I know. He went from the victim having hot water thrown on his body, causing severe burns, to smiling and speaking with such wisdom.

The victorious survivor is a light for his generation. In such a time as this, I envision him speaking at teen summits, interviewing with some famous talk show hosts. I admire the relationship he has with his father. Clearly, you can see the love, strength, and affection shown as they feed off each other. His father instilled morals and values into his son. To respect others and to demand respect.

The victorious survivor adores and believes in the word of God. Therefore, to know this young man is to love him. He is a constant reminder that regardless of what life brings, remember to smile, be happy, and sing your song.

How did the testimony of this overcomer touch your heart, and can you relate?

_____

_____

_____

What was your first impression of the visual IAE portrait? What is it saying to you, and how does it make you feel?

_____

_____

_____

What lesson(s) did you learn?

_____

_____

_____

How can you use this testimony to understand, find your purpose, or continue your walk with Christ?

_____

_____

[CHAPTER 6]— THE MIRACLE WORKER

This woman is so full of life and dear to my heart. She is my sister-in-love, the wife of my second to the oldest brother. God endowed her with a cheerful and caring personality. However, in her story, on Martin Luther King Jr. Day, riding with her husband and son, they were in a bad car accident. While on the way to a church banquet in honor of Martin Luther King Jr., they hit a patch of black ice, wrecked, and the car wrapped around a giant tree. The impact of the wreck left my sister-in-love in a coma and brain damage. Her husband and son experienced minor injuries.

After the accident, my sister-in-love developed a new outlook on life. She is no longer a people-pleaser. Sometimes we try to protect others' feelings instead of protecting our own. She realized her well-being is just as important as the needs of other people. Nevertheless, in the reality of it all, she had to be at peace with herself. God wants us to live our lives the way HE created, unique, and wonderfully made. We are all different, and that is perfectly *ok*. The world needs our differences to make it a better place. So, let your light shine bright and unapologetically. My sister-in-love inspires me to operate in the spirit of excellence no matter what my limitations may be. Despite life's difficulties, keep pushing. With God, all things are possible. Live in every moment, pay attention to everyone around you, and love on people hard. Finally, fall in love with God repeatedly, and watch for the signs.

IAE PORTRAIT

During the Photoshoot, The Miracle Worker and I envisioned her the same.

First image – We saw her in a hospital gown with her hair covered and looking in the mirror with uncertainty. She wanted all the words written in the mirror describing how she saw herself. People-pleaser, lonely, comatose, tired, and separated. These words describe the feelings throughout her life, during the accident, and the brain injury. She has a praying husband who watched and cared intently for her. Daily anointing and speaking to God on her behalf. A priest indeed and a mighty man of valor. Finally, she learned to walk again and how to care for her daily needs.

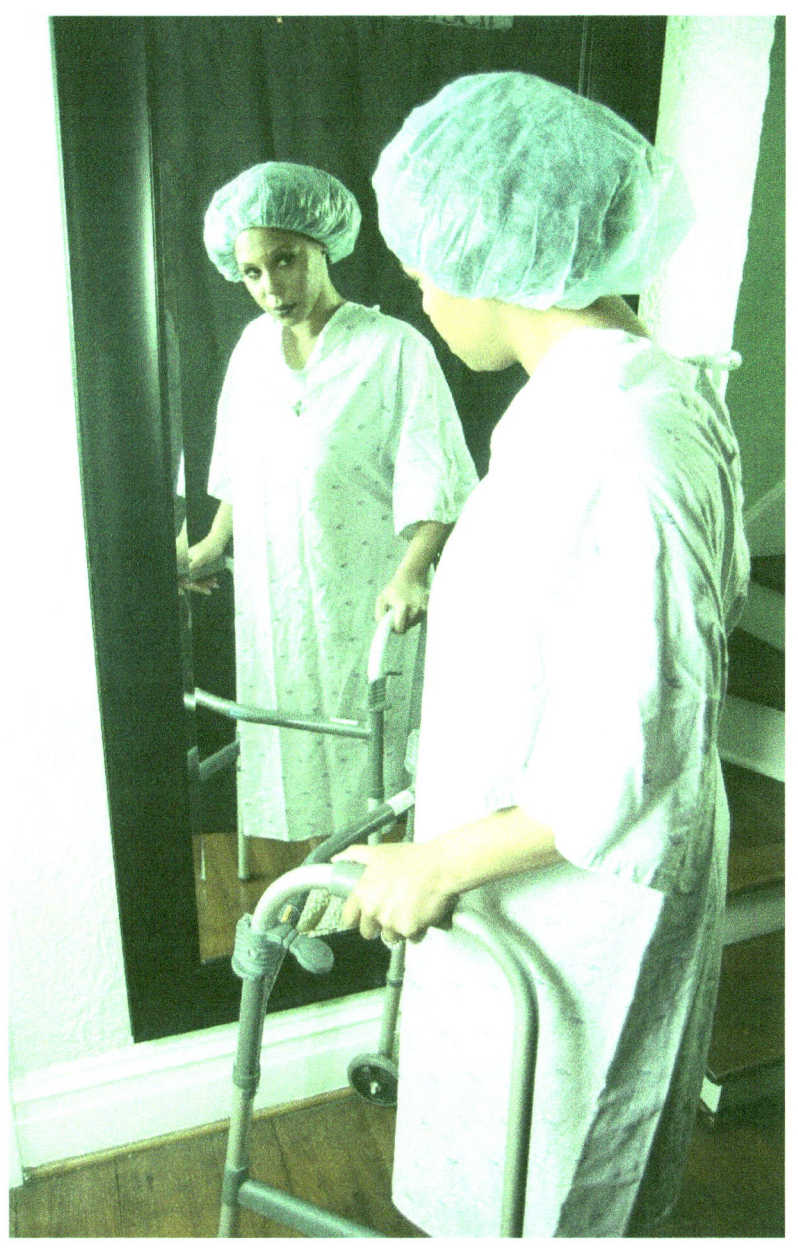

Second image – Standing strong with an extended arm making a muscle. Indicating the strength of God and excitement about her new life. She wears a shirt that says it all, "Yet becoming!" Becoming who God created her to be. Before our session ended, these words came to mind, full of laughter, beauty, confidence, and grace. As before, I believe she will continue educating and inspiring the youth Uplifting quotes, affirmations, and gospel music aided in the healing process. Sayings like, "If God brings you to it, and HE will carry you through it." The inspirational song "Fill me up" is one of her favorites, and anecdotes such as "A goal without a plan is just a wish."

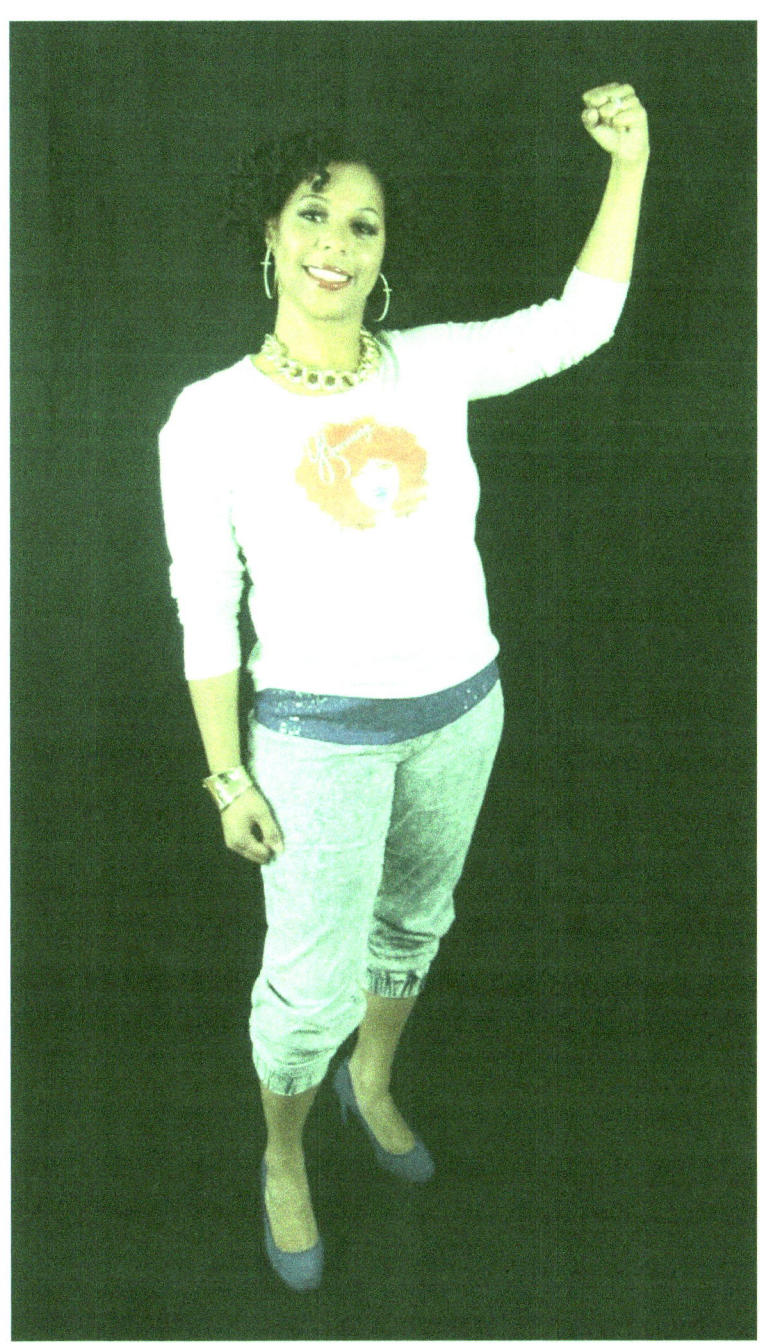

After her recovery, in 2015, The Miracle Worker and her husband started the company "Youth Innovations." Helping the youth defy the odds after school program. The program far exceeded their expectations; it has grown each year since the beginning.

Her story is a testament to the greatness of God in our lives. God sustained their life through it all. The dream of The Miracle Worker is finally birthed to fruition. When she graduated college, and before the accident, she dreamed of having a family, starting the youth program to build a legacy, and giving hope. Dreams fulfilled, and nothing deferred. The Miracle Worker birthed three babies, and the last one is a miracle. The success of the youth innovations after school program helped some of the community youths beat the odds. The Miracle Worker and family live a life of gratitude, love, and passion for their children and others. Children succeeding and defying the odds of society is the intended goal.

ANGEL NURSE and the miracle worker

In the story of The Miracle Worker, I had the opportunity to speak with her husband, my brother. He mentioned an angel on earth in the form of a nurse who cared for the Miracle Worker during her hospital stay. He described the nurse with beautiful melanin skin and shiny grey hair. Her husband reminded me angels still exist.

I could picture the angel nurse gently rubbing my sister-in love's hair and caring for her. Reminiscent of the fact God is real. He is just as alive and prevalent in the lives of His people today as back then. The existence of angels is essential in helping to carry out God's messages. I can call on them in prayer to protect, lead and guide me in this world today. The bible says, "God will give HIS angels charge over me."

My brother and sister-in-love went back to the hospital to thank the nurse for taking such good care of her. However, the hospital had no record of her ever-having employment there… (Praise break!) God is Omnipotent and truly amazing!

How did the testimony of this overcomer touch your heart, and can you relate?

_____

_____

_____

What was your first impression of the visual IAE portrait? What is it saying to you, and how does it make you feel?

_____

_____

_____

What lesson(s) did you learn?

_____

_____

_____

How can you use this testimony to understand, find your purpose, or continue your walk with Christ?

_____

_____

[CHAPTER 7]— THE HUSBAND OF FAITH

The moment I met the husband of faith, he appeared to be a great husband. Right away, I discerned the love he had for his wife while telling his story. I saw how eager and badly he wanted to be a great provider and take away her worries. In 2014, the husband of faith had a stroke. Battling with his health and deficits from the stroke, he had to relearn motor skills and restore his faith in God. The husband of faith felt as though God, whom he served, left him alone when he needed HIM the most.

The husband of faith did not want his wife to worry or go through any pains. However, she was just as concerned for him as he was for her. Therefore, the husband of faith's wife, submitting herself to God, turns her face to the wall praying for her husband's healing. Desperate needs call for desperate measures. Hezekiah, in the bible, did the exact thing. First, he turned his face to the wall and met with God. Then remind God of his faithfulness. Then proceeded to ask God for what he needed. God responded by honoring Hezekiah's request and adding more years to his life.

I adored their bond and spirit for one another. True love. The minority community would refer to them as black love, meaning true excellence of a king and queen. I learned through their testimony to cherish your spouse and not take each other for granted. Be intentional about the time you spend together, building one another. Continue strengthening and growing your marriage. The husband of faith's wife made a statement that stuck with me, "Less is more, and the little things are valued."

God is not complicated; He is simple. However, we make things more complex than they are. Doing things God's way makes life easier. Spend time with HIM and develop a relationship so you can hear him clearly about your life. A union under God requires the husband and wife to pray for each other in marriage. You are a team. The husband, the priest of the home, covers the family as they pour into each other. Working together through this thing called life. Marriage is sacred. Lifting, not tearing down. A beautiful union designed to bring glory to God is its purpose.

God's word helped the husband of faith heal. "*Trust in the Lord with all thine heart and lean not unto thine own understanding. In all thy ways acknowledge him, and he shall direct thy path.* **Proverbs 3: 5, 6 KJV.** Faith shaken and doubting God, he continued reading the bible. Going through the unknown periods in our lives, we must trust God and believe in HIS plan. I am inspired to stay in tune with my body, physically, exercising, eating healthy, mentally, and spiritually. Self-care is essential; we cannot be all we need to be for our families if we do not care for ourselves first.

IAE Photoshoot

During the IAE photoshoot

First image – I envisioned the husband of faith in a hospital gown, sitting in a wheelchair. Head down in sadness, fear, disappointment, and losing faith in God.

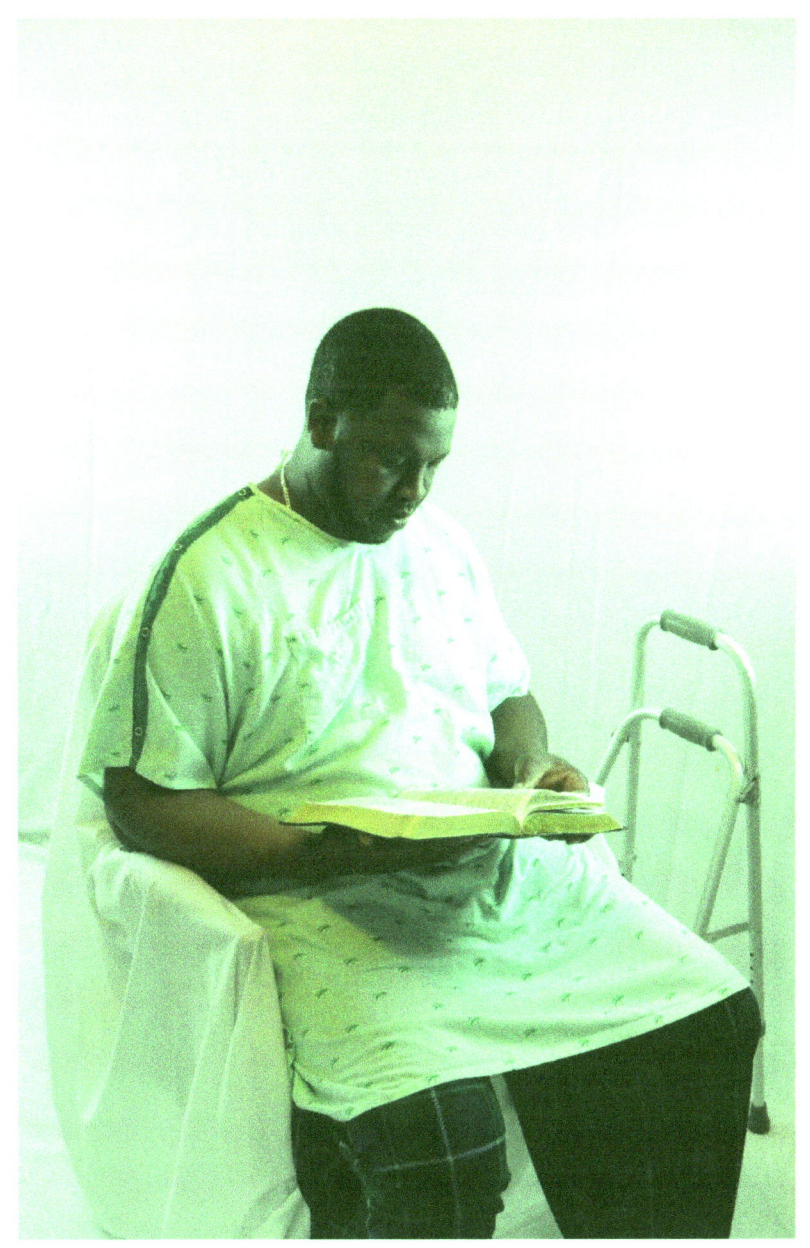

Second image – I saw him standing. Leaning on the wheelchair, looking up to God with renewed faith, thanking HIM for his life. Gospel and quartet musical groups got the husband of faith through his ordeal.

IAE…THE PHOTOGRAPHY PROCESS

Why photography? How did you get into photography? People ask this question a lot. The answer is simple; God gave it to me. When searching for my purpose, I heard someone say, "Our true purpose as believers in Christ is serving, worshipping, and testifying about God's word to unbelievers." Photography is an avenue gifted to me to carry out HIS mission. Each photoshoot is purposeful. God evolved my childhood hobby into a passion, and from there to purpose.

I loved posing for the camera; I have a box full of pictures to prove it. However, I remember a picture of myself wearing a red and black striped Michael Jackson jacket, holding a deer horn in my hand. This picture makes my heart smile every time I see it.

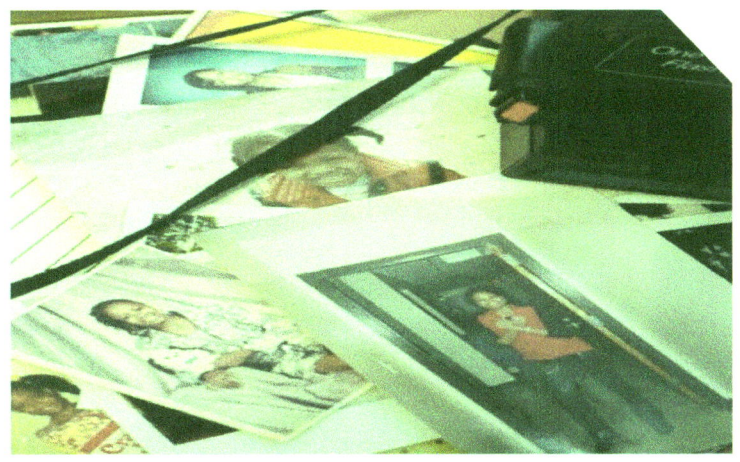

My parents already knew the gift inside me. I just did not recognize it until now. Taking pictures back in my early days came naturally to me. I did not think anything of it. I had a box full of photos that captured accomplishments with friends and classmates and youth experiences. My dad loved editing wedding videos and creating voice-overs for radio.

My style and paying attention to detail comes from my mom. Therefore, undoubtedly, I inherited this photography gift, embedded in me, from my parents. If only I had asked God before making my own decisions about what path to take for my life. I could have avoided many things, such as the post-partum depression I suffered after giving birth. Much wiser now, perhaps I had to go through those years to get me where I am today.

My journey humbled me, and I appreciate the gift that gave me my purpose. Along the way, I lost the adventurous side that I fought to get back to…but without God, I could not do it. Once I let go, I started to see the vision and watched God blow my mind! God aligns us with people who can bless and bring us into your future. Pay attention to the signs.

My friends enjoy every minute of your life. Live in your purpose and inspire others to do the same.

THE JOURNEY OF GETTING TO KNOW ME

-My Nineteen-Year-Old Self-

To the nineteen-year-old girl,

You are about to go through the challenge of your life. Here are the tools you will need...prayer, salvation, and God's plan. Follow through with the plan and never lose your joy in the process, no matter how hard it may seem. Keep living and soar into the powerful woman God created.

"Prayer for my gift"

Dear God,

Help me to remember the natural gifts given to me as a child. The things that came easy to me without trying. Ignite in me again, the same passion I once had for my gift. In addition, God, once you have revealed the gift or gifts, provide the angels on earth and the resources to develop the skill set to soar in my gifts. God, I had a plan for my life; however, I know your goal is much better. Therefore, I surrender, and I will let you lead the way from now on. God, forgive me for doing life my way. I love you and thank you for another chance to get it right.

In Jesus name,

Amen

"Prayer for salvation"

Dear God,

Forgive me for the unknown sins and for the sins known. I surrender my life to you. I want to follow you and live life your way. I want salvation and the joy of daily unconditional love. I believe in the Father, Son, and Holy Ghost. I believe Jesus, Your Son, died for our sins and rose again on the third day, so I can be saved and truly live once again. Lord, please lead and guide me in this new journey every step of the way. Give me discernment of the people and places I should go from this day forward. I trust YOU with my life. I love you! Thank YOU, God, for saving me.

In Jesus name,

Amen

The journey of getting to know me:

1. What am I naturally passionate about? What makes me smile and have joy when I think about it?

2. What am I good at without trying?

3. What are my strengths?

4. What are my favorite colors, food, and my place to visit?

This week take the time to begin the journey of getting to know the "real" you. Use the IAE journal to write everything you discover about yourself. Remember, you are constantly evolving. Embrace every moment of your life! Now that you have found everything that brings you joy make it your business to do them often. I love you, and God loves you too. Go live the abundant life as promised.

Sincerely,

The Purpose Seeker!

JOURNAL NOTES

MORE IAE INSPIRATIONS/LIFE LESSONS

Job 23 decrees:

- ➢ He performs the things appointed for me.
- ➢ He performs what is planned for me.
- ➢ He will certainly accomplish what he decreed for me.
- ➢ He is mindful of many such things.
- ➢ He will do to me whatever he has planned, and He controls my destiny.

Isaiah 43:

- ➢ Fear not, for I am with you.
- ➢ When you pass through the waters, I will be with thee; they shall not overflow thee.
- ➢ When you walk through the fire; you shall not be burned.
- ➢ I will make a way in the wilderness, and rivers in the desert.

   Prepare – Succeed – Establish and Become!

2Kings 3:

➢ **Victory has strategy.**

➢ **God has a solution for you to win; it is not always popular.**

➢ **Whatever God said, it is already settled.**

Facts to Ponder:

➢ **God will take your broken pieces and make you whole.**

➢ **God will blot out your transgressions for His own sake and will not remember your sins.**

➢ **God will give water to the thirsty.**

➢ **God will pour out His spirit upon your children, and**

➢ **His blessing upon your offspring.**

➢ **In the day of calamity, the Lord is your trust.**

Remember, the Lord formed thee from your mother's womb. God chose our paths before we were born. He makes all things for us to accomplish our missions.

The Family

-Finding my place-

-The Mitchell Girls-

-Vision Manifested-

-Confidence-

Dreams Fulfilled

Mr. and Mrs. Mitchell

Advertisement-in the beginning.

Introducing a New Project

called "The IVT Movement "of Healing,
Deliverance, & Salvation for the Individual
and for the world we live in today!

The Inspirational Visual Testimony (IVT)
formally known as the IAE (Inspirational
Alter-Ego) Is a sense of Freedom, Peace,
Joy, Living in Your Purpose, and Inspiring
others to do the same!

Description: 2 Powerful Images; one of a
person's struggle or turning point in life,
and another pose of who they are now,
their victory.

Contact: Amillion & 1 Photography and
Video Imaging at 803-216-5190 or @
www.amillionand1.com

For your opportunity to Inspire the World !

~Blessings

Ebony M.

Isaiah 40:31

But they that wait upon
the Lord shall renew their strength:
they shall mount up with wings as eagles:
they shall run, and not be weary: and
they shall walk, and not faint.

THE IAE MOVEMENT CONTINUES:

We receive healing, deliverance, and salvation when we tell our own stories. If you feel the unction because I believe God leads people to you, contact us to envision your Inspirational Alter-Ego. I am so excited for you; I get joy just thinking about your healing taking place through your journey. Our location is in Lancaster, S.C. To contact us, call 803-216-5190 or www.amillion1.com. Stay connected with us through instagram@amillion1photographyvideo, on Facebook Amillion&1Photography, and talk with the author of the IAE.

YouTube has the full interview of the overcomers' stories

Steps for those interested:

A consultation is given, and the overcomer tells their testimony. Before and mainly during the photoshoot, God provides the photographer with visual direction. Her gifts of discernment from the spiritual aspect come alive. She begins by seeing and feeling, very keen and detailed, and positioning the subject based on their story.

Each photo shoot starts with a prayer asking God to lead and guide us to display His will and bring each person's testimony to life. Therefore, the world can understand, the movement is of God, and He gets all the glory. The overcomers' favorite song plays, family, and friends can come in for support. The photoshoot is a part of the healing process, deliverance, and manifesting breakthrough.

Overcomers will leave the photoshoot feeling happy, joyful, carefree, and at peace, excited to share their story with the world. So, if someone else going through the same thing or something similar, they have strength to refocus. Now readers can have a visual journey they can relate to and know whatever they face is only temporary. Seeing other overcomers survive and are stronger for it.

I encourage you to find someone to share your emotions with; talk it out with a friend. Nevertheless, whatever the challenge, do not suffer in silence. The Inspirational Alter-Ego Movement maintains itself as an outlet readily available to anyone. A no-shade thrown zone. Every person needs to hear how incredible he or she are, even with battle scars. The Visual testimonial portrait allows me to see your value, so I can show you your worth. There is so much beauty underneath the pain. The camera lens will bring to the surface the king or queen in you.

FINAL THOUGHTS...

At the end of the day, I learned and experienced things I never thought I would. Yet I endured my trials because giving up was not an option. I, Ebony Mitchell, had to survive. Following Christ is a mandate. You must listen, ask questions, and HE will lead you daily. For my yoke is easy, and my burden is light. **Matthew 11:30 KJV.**

I pray I inspired you (the reader) to continue your journey. Then, if the need ever arises, begin again with wings as Eagles.

Ebony

The End

ABOUT THE AUTHOR

Ebony Mitchell was born and raised in the small-town of Lancaster, South Carolina. She is a very adventurous and optimistic person who loves family hard, travels, writes, & does her best to enjoy every minute of her life that God has given her. Her motivation to finish writing this book was to heal internally so that her daughter's wouldn't have to and to truly live in her purpose and inspire others to do the same. Ebony is a wife to Nicholas Mitchell who out of love created 4 beautiful daughters, Lyrik, Destiny Maleah, Emori, & Joy. Through her life's journey she graduated from South Carolina State University where she obtained a Bachelor's Degree in Biology with a minor in Chemistry. She attended the Doctorate of Chiropractic school where she fell in love with anatomy, taught middle school science, and then started her Business Amillion & 1 Photography & Video Imaging. Ebony feels that in life you're always evolving, and she is excited to see what next Big Idea God will reveal in her life. Ebony's hope is that by reading this book you will start the journey of gaining the knowledge of who you are, and to truly become exactly who God created you to be!

www.ingramcontent.com/pod-product-compliance
Lightning Source LLC
Chambersburg PA
CBHW051548120626
46551CB00013B/1418